Contents

INTRODUCTION

The cardiac food plan is an ingesting plan that let you reduce the impact of your weight loss program for your heart health. The ordinary purpose is to reduce sodium and fat intake. Too an awful lot sodium can increase your blood pressure, leading to hypertension. Hypertension is a prime threat component for coronary heart attacks and different heart issues. Fat, on the other hand, can cause plaque to build up on your artery partitions, also main to coronary heart disorder.

Other names for the cardiac weight-reduction plan include the heart-wholesome weight loss program, the low-sodium weight-reduction plan, and the DASH food regimen. (DASH stands for dietary procedures to prevent hypertension.)

This book contains all the necessary benefits of cardiac diet and cookbook of different recipes to try.

WHAT IS THE CARDIAC DIET

The cardiac food plan is an ingesting plan that let you reduce the impact of your weight loss program for your heart health. The ordinary purpose is to reduce sodium and fat intake. Too an awful lot sodium can increase your blood pressure, leading to hypertension. Hypertension is a prime threat component for coronary heart attacks and different heart issues. Fat, on the other hand, can cause plaque to build up on your artery partitions, also main to coronary heart disorder.

Other names for the cardiac weight-reduction plan include the heart-wholesome weight loss program, the low-sodium weight-reduction plan, and the DASH food regimen. (DASH stands for dietary procedures to prevent hypertension.)

ARE THERE OTHER NAMES FOR THIS WEIGHT LOSS PROGRAM?

Other names for the cardiac weight-reduction plan include the heart-wholesome weight loss program, the low-sodium weight-reduction plan, and the DASH food regimen. (DASH stands for dietary procedures to prevent hypertension.)

HOW CAN A CARDIAC DIET HELP SOMEONE WITH CANCER?

Cancer treatments can lead to short-term and lengthy-term coronary heart issues. The cardiac weight-reduction plan is useful for people who are looking to control high blood pressure, reduce their blood ldl cholesterol degree, or decrease their hazard of coronary heart disease.

WHAT ARE THE PRIMARY HINTS OF THE CARDIAC FOOD PLAN?

Here are a few hints that let you avoid fats and sodium:

- No extra than 25 to 35 percent of your daily energy should come from general fat (this includes saturated fat).

- Less than 7 percentage of your daily calories should come from saturated fats.

- Avoid trans fat.

- Consume less than 2 hundred milligrams a day of nutritional cholesterol.

- Limit your salt consumption; goal for much less than 2 grams of sodium consistent with day or less

- Drink alcohol in moderation: one serving in line with day for ladies and two in step with day for guys. (One serving is same to twelve oz of beer, 5 oz of wine, and 1.Five oz. Of distilled spirits.)

WHAT ARE THE MEALS YOU COULD CONSUME AT THE CARDIAC EATING REGIMEN?

FOOD GROUPS	FOODS TO INCLUDE
Milk and Dairy Products	Fat-free or 1 percentage milk, yogurt, or cottage cheese
	Fat-loose and coffee-fat cheese
Vegetables	All fresh greens
	All frozen veggies
	Low-sodium canned vegetables (have to be drained and rinsed)

Fruit and Juices	All clean fruit
	All frozen fruit
Breads and Grains	Whole-wheat products, which include bread, pasta, crackers, and cereals
	Brown rice
	Oats
	Quinoa
	Barley
	Low-fat crackers and pretzels
	Plain air-popped popcorn

Meats and Other Proteins

Lean cuts of pork and red meat (loin, leg, spherical, and further-lean ground meat)

Skinless poultry

Fish

Venison and different wild game

Dried beans and peas

Nuts and nut butters

Meat options made

with soy or textured

vegetable protein

Egg whites or egg

replacement

Cold cuts made with

lean meat or soy protein

Fats and Oils   Unsaturated oils

(olive, peanut, soy, sunflower, and canola)

Soft or liquid

margarines and vegetable

oil spreads

Salad dressings

Seeds and nuts	Avocados
Beverages	Water
	Sparkling water
	Tea
	Coffee

WHAT ARE THE MEALS TO KEEP AWAY FROM ON THE CARDIAC DIET?

If you are following the cardiac diet, the main foods to observe are salt and saturated fats.

Saturated fat are typically animal-based totally sources of fat, which includes butter and lard.

FOOD GROUPS

AVOID

Milk and Dairy Products

Whole milk

2 percent

milk

Whole-milk

yogurt or ice cream

Cream

Half-and-half

of Cream cheese

Sour cream

Cheese

Vegetables

FOODS TO

Fried greens

Vegetables

organized with

butter, cheese, or a

cream sauce

Fruit and Juices   Fried fruits

Fruits served

with butter or cream

Breads and Grains   High-fats

bakery merchandise,

including doughnuts,

biscuits, croissants,

pastries, pies, and

cookies

Snacks made

with partially

hydrogenated oils,

together with chips,

cheese puffs, snack

mixes, everyday

crackers, and butter-

flavored popcorn

Meats and Other Proteins   Higher-fats

cuts of meat (ribs, T-

bone steak, and

normal ground

meat)

William

Maxwell Aitken

Sausage

Cold cuts, inclusive of salami or bologna

Corned pork

Hot dogs

Organ meats (liver, brains, and sweetbreads)

Poultry with skin

Fried meat, rooster, and fish

Whole eggs

and egg yolks

Fats and Oils   Butter

margarine

Stick

Shortening

Partially

hydrogenated oils

Tropical oils

(coconut, palm, and

palm kernel)

If you have got been prescribed a blood thinner, which include warfarin (Coumadin®, Jantoven®), make sure to devour meals wealthy in diet K on a daily basis. This will assist prevent blood clots and bleeding. Leafy inexperienced veggies, such as kale, spinach, and collards, are the first-rate sources of nutrition K. For greater statistics on vitamin K and blood thinners, ask your health practitioner or dietitian.

WHAT ARE SOME COMMON LAWSUITS FROM HUMANS ON THE CARDIAC DIET, AND THE WAY DO YOU CLEAR UP THEM?

The maximum commonplace criticism amongst humans on the cardiac diet is the lack of salt. Fortunately, there are a number of ways you can enhance the taste of your meals with out the need for sodium.

Here are a few tips:

- A burst of acidity can brighten a dish. Try lemon juice, lime juice, and vinegar.

- Dry or sparkling herbs upload taste. Try basil, bay leaf, dill, rosemary, parsley, sage, dry mustard, nutmeg, thyme, and paprika. You can also purchase a sodium-

loose seasoning mixture or make your
very own at home.

- Black pepper, red pepper flakes, and
cayenne pepper can spice up your meals
with out adding sodium. Hot sauce
includes sodium, however if you use only
a drop or , it'll no longer add up to a
whole lot.

MAKE YOUR VERY OWN SEASONING COMBINATION

Here's a blend of seasonings you may use whilst
trying to cut returned on salt. This makes about
1/3 cup.

- 5 teaspoons onion powder

- 2½ teaspoons garlic powder

- 2½ teaspoons paprika

- 2½ teaspoon dry mustard

- 1½ teaspoon beaten thyme leaves

- ½ teaspoon white pepper

- ¼ teaspoon celery seed

WHAT ARE A FEW HINTS FOR HUMAN BEINGS ON THE CARDIAC EATING REGIMEN?

Choose heart-healthful carbohydrates.

- Increase your viscous (soluble) fiber consumption with meals together with

Brussels sprouts, sweet potatoes, turnips,

apricots, mangoes, oranges, legumes,

barley, oats, and oat bran. Aim for 5 to 10

grams day by day. As you boom your fiber

intake progressively, additionally increase

the quantity of water you drink. This will

assist you avoid troubles with gas.

- Limit refined carbohydrates, together

  with desk sugar, chocolates, and

  beverages sweetened with delivered

  sugar.

- Decrease saturated fats through selecting lean protein and coffee-fats dairy merchandise.

- Monounsaturated fats and omega-3 polyunsaturated fat are precise to your coronary heart's health. Choose nuts, avocados, olives, or olive oil to get monounsaturated fat. Use canola, soybean, or walnut oil to get omega-3 fat.

Reduce fats through your protein selections.

- Bake, broil, roast, stew, or stir-fry very lean cuts of red meat or red meat, such as those categorised "loin" or "round," in addition to fish and rooster.

- Take the pores and skin off chicken (inclusive of chook or turkey) earlier than serving it.

- Get protein from plant foods (which include soy, dried beans and legumes, nuts, and seeds) or egg whites in place of meat.

Cut lower back on sodium.

- Cook meals at domestic to take price of the salt content in what you devour.

- When you buy canned goods, pick no-sodium or low-sodium alternatives.

- Use as little salt in cooking as feasible. You can cut as a minimum half of the salt from maximum recipes.

CAN I USE SALT SUBSTITUTES ON THE CARDIAC WEIGHT-REDUCTION PLAN?

Check together with your physician earlier than using any salt substitutes. These products include massive amounts of potassium that your health practitioner won't need you to have. In particular, people with kidney issues or those taking potassium-sparing diuretics want to take care with potassium. Other salt substitutes, together with Mrs. Dash, do now not incorporate potassium and are safe for all people.

Phrases like "low sodium" and "decreased saturated fats" seek advice from precise measurements. Here's a key to knowledge the ones phrases:

- Sodium unfastened or salt loose way much less than five milligrams of sodium.

- Very low sodium approach 35 milligrams of sodium or much less.

- Low sodium approach 140 milligrams of sodium of less.

- Reduced sodium approach at the least 25 percentage much less sodium than the ordinary product (watch out as the sodium content material may also nevertheless be excessive).

- Light in sodium manner as a minimum 50 percent much less sodium than the overall-sodium product.

Saturated fats claims:

How do I realize what foods are the proper quantity of salt or saturated fats? Here are some tips for studying saturated fat labels.

- Saturated fats loose way much less than 0.5 grams of saturated fats and much less than zero.5 grams of trans fatty acids.

- Low in saturated fats approach 1 gram of saturated fat or much less and no more than 15 percent energy from saturated fat.

- Reduced saturated fat method at least 25 percentage less saturated fat and decreased via more than 1 gram of fats in comparison with the whole-fat product.

- Try and pick out meals with less than 5 grams of total fat according to serving, less than 2 grams of saturated fats per serving, and 0 grams of trans fats according to serving.

When at a restaurant, don't hesitate to make special requests. Here are some tips:

- Choose entrées, potatoes, and greens organized without sauces, cheese, or butter (or ask for them at the aspect).

- Eat a small portion of meat. Fill up on greens.

- Avoid such toppings as crumbled bacon or cheese.

- Ask for smooth margarine or olive oil instead of butter.

- Select ingredients which might be
  steamed, broiled, baked, roasted, or stir-
  fried.

CARDIAC DIET COOKBOOK

BLACK BEANS, CORN, AND QUINOA SALAD

Ingredients

- ½ cup crimson quinoa

- 1 cup water

- 15-ounce can black beans (1¾ cup
  cooked)

- 15.25-ounce can corn, drained

- 1 medium crimson bell pepper, diced

- 1 cup cherry tomatoes, halved

- 2 cloves garlic, minced

- 6 tablespoons extra-virgin olive oil

- four tablespoons lime juice

- 1 teaspoon lime zest

- ½ cup sparkling cilantro, chopped

- ¼ teaspoon salt

- 1 avocado, diced

Instructions

- Thoroughly rinse sparkling produce under warm running water for 20 seconds. Scrub to put off excess dirt.

- Rinse quinoa in a excellent-mesh colander below going for walks water for at the least 30 seconds. Drain nicely.

- In a saucepan, convey rinsed quinoa and water to a boil over medium-high warmness, then lessen warmth and simmer until quinoa has absorbed the liquid, 10 to twelve minutes. Remove pan from warmness, cover, and let stand 5 minutes.

- When quinoa is cool, add it to a huge bowl with beans, corn, bell pepper, tomatoes, garlic, olive oil, lime juice and zest, cilantro, and salt and blend well.

Cover and kick back for some hours or in a single day.

- To serve, bring salad to room temperature, add avocado, and blend lightly to mix.

- Washing the quinoa nicely before cooking helps to remove bitterness because of certainly occurring saponins. Saponins are chemicals found in quinoa and different plant-based meals, and had been shown to own a number of fitness blessings.

BUTTERNUT SQUASH AND APPLE SOUP

This creamy, easy-to-swallow soup makes for the final heart-wholesome consolation food. The

greater intensity of flavor comes from roasting
the squash and then letting the soup simmer for
30 minutes after blending.

Ingredients

- 2½ cups butternut squash, peeled and
  cubed

- 4 tablespoons extra-virgin olive oil

- 1 yellow onion, chopped

- 1 clove garlic, minced

- 5 cups low-sodium vegetable stock

- 2 cups water

- 1 sixteen-ounce can pumpkin puree

- 2 medium crimson apples, peeled and
  chopped

- ¼ teaspoon ground cinnamon

- ¼ teaspoon ground nutmeg

- ¼ teaspoon ground cloves

- ¼ teaspoon salt

- ½ teaspoon black pepper

- 4 tablespoons low-fat plain Greek yogurt

- Roasted pumpkin seeds (non-obligatory)

Instructions

- Thoroughly rinse sparkling produce below heat running water for 20 seconds. Scrub to get rid of extra dust.

- Preheat oven to 350 levels.

- Line a rimmed baking sheet with parchment paper, then unfold squash

evenly on paper. Drizzle squash with 2
tablespoons olive oil and roast eight to 10
minutes. Remove from oven and set
apart.

- Heat closing 2 tablespoons olive oil in a
  huge pot over medium warmness. Add
  onion and garlic. Cook until onion is
  tender and begins to brown. Add roasted
  squash, vegetable inventory, water,
  pumpkin puree, apples, cinnamon,
  nutmeg, cloves, salt, and black pepper.
  Bring to a boil over excessive warmth,
  then reduce to a simmer and cook till
  squash and apples are soft, about 20

minutes. Remove from warmness and
permit cool.

- Puree soup using an immersion blender,
  meals mill, food processor, or blender.
  Place pot over low warmth till soup is
  warmed via, about half-hour. Add yogurt,
  stirring till completely mixed. Soup need
  to be one hundred forty five levels the use
  of an instantaneous-read thermometer.

- Ladle soup into bowls and garnish with
  seeds, if using.

CANTALOUPE AND MINT GRANITA

Originating in Sicily, granitas are just like Italian

ice. They're additionally heart healthier than ice

cream and so easy to make. This fresh version
combines the creamy sweetness of cantaloupe
with the tang of lime and mint.

Ingredients

- 2 cups water

- 1 cup sugar, or more to flavor

- 1¼ cup sparkling mint leaves

- 1 cantaloupe, peeled, seeded, and
  chopped

- three tablespoons lime juice

Instructions

- Thoroughly rinse clean produce beneath
  warm running water for 20 seconds. Scrub
  to cast off excess dust.

- In a small saucepan, combine the water, 1 cup sugar, and 1 cup mint leaves. Bring to a boil over medium warmth. Reduce warmness and simmer, stirring once in a while, till sugar has dissolved, approximately five mins. Remove pan from warmth and set apart to chill, approximately 20 mins. Pour cooled syrup thru a strainer to dispose of mint leaves.
- In a blender, puree the strained syrup, cantaloupe, and lime juice till smooth, then taste. To sweeten greater, add 1 tablespoon sugar at a time and blend; flavor and repeat until desired flavor is

reached. Add remaining mint leaves and blend till finely chopped.

- Pour the combination into a 9x13 glass baking dish and freeze, as a minimum 8 hours or overnight.

- Using the tines of a fork, scrape the granita to the preferred texture and serve in chilled bowls.

CAULIFLOWER RICE WITH SAUTÉED VEGETABLES

Even even though it's low in fats, this cauliflower rice side dish is hearty. To keep time, use frozen cauliflower rice.

Ingredients

- 5 cups cauliflower florets (approximately 1½ heads cauliflower)

- 1 tablespoon olive oil

- 1 teaspoon minced garlic

- ½ pink bell pepper, coarsely chopped into 1-inch pieces

- ½ yellow bell pepper, coarsely chopped into 1-inch pieces

- ½ zucchini, coarsely chopped into 1-inch portions

- ½ yellow summer squash, coarsely chopped into 1-inch portions

- Salt and pepper

- 2 tablespoons bird broth

Instructions

- Thoroughly rinse fresh produce below heat walking water for 20 seconds. Scrub to put off extra dust, then set aside.

- Place cauliflower in a meals processor and pulse numerous times till cauliflower resembles rice.

- Heat olive oil in a big skillet over medium-excessive warmth. Add garlic and stir till fragrant, about 1 minute. Add bell peppers, zucchini, and squash. Season with salt and pepper to taste. Cook till vegetables start to soften, stirring now and again, about 5 to 7 minutes. Add cauliflower rice and hen broth and stir properly, until chicken stick reduces via

1/2 and veggies are absolutely cooked.

Internal temperature of cauliflower rice

need to be one hundred forty five degrees

using an instant-examine thermometer.

CHICKEN TAMALE PIE

This casserole dish, made with a sprinkling of

low-fat cheddar, relies on taste in place of fats or

salt. Incorporating more salt-free seasonings into

your cooking can assist while you're seeking to

observe a cardiac eating regimen.

Ingredients

- ½ cup cornmeal

- 2 cups low-sodium chook broth

- Cooking spray

- 1 to two cups of baked hen, shredded

- 1 cup low-sodium tomato sauce

- 1 teaspoon garlic powder

- 1 teaspoon oregano

- 1 teaspoon thyme

- ¼ cup low-fat cheddar cheese, grated

- Fresh cilantro (non-obligatory)

Instructions

- Preheat oven to 350 degrees.

- Combine cornmeal and chicken broth in a medium saucepan and prepare dinner over medium warmth, stirring frequently, till aggregate thickens. Let cool 5 minutes.

- Lightly coat a small casserole dish with cooking spray.

- Spread cornmeal combination on bottom of casserole dish to create a base.

- Spread shredded fowl on pinnacle of cornmeal.

- Place tomato sauce in a small bowl and stir within the garlic powder, oregano, and thyme. Evenly distribute the tomato sauce over the hen.

- Sprinkle with grated cheese.

- Bake for 30 minutes or until cheese melts.

- Garnish with fresh cilantro if desired.

CRANBERRY-STUFFED CHICKEN BREASTS

This tart and tangy chook dish is full of healthful

protein with out being brief on taste.

Ingredients

- 1½ tablespoons plus 1 teaspoon olive oil

- 1 small apple, peeled and diced

- ½ cup dried cranberries

- 1 shallot, peeled and diced

- ¾ cup low-sodium chook inventory

- four boneless, skinless bird breasts, about

  four to six oz each

- ¼ cup balsamic vinegar

- Salt and pepper

Instructions

- Heat 1 teaspoon olive oil in a skillet over medium-excessive warmness. Add apple and cook till tender, three to 4 mins.

- In a small bowl, combine cooked apple, cranberries, shallot, and 1 tablespoon bird inventory. Set aside.

- Cut a deep horizontal pocket within the side of every chicken breast. Make the pocket as big as you may with out piercing the pinnacle or bottom of the breast. Divide apple combination lightly amongst chook breasts, stuffing into each pocket. Secure wallet with toothpicks, threading along the side to shut.

- Heat ultimate 1½ tablespoons olive oil in a heavy skillet. Cook fowl, turning once, till golden brown. Add vinegar and ultimate hen inventory, then carry to a boil. Lower warmth and lightly simmer bird, turning as soon as, 2 or 3 minutes per aspect.

- When hen registers 165 stages Fahrenheit or better the usage of an on the spot-study thermometer placed in the thickest a part of the breast, remove from skillet and hold warm.

- Continue cooking sauce till decreased to a thick syrup. Season with salt and pepper to taste.

- Spoon sauce over chook to serve.

EDAMAME HUMMUS

This hummus is in reality scrumptious. Packed with protein, edamame makes the ideal snack when you want a midday raise.

Ingredients

- 2 cups frozen shelled edamame

- 2 tablespoons tahini

- 2 cloves garlic, peeled

- 2 tablespoons olive oil

- 1 tablespoon cilantro leaves

- Juice of 2 lemons

- Salt and pepper

Instructions

- Thoroughly rinse fresh produce under warm walking water for 20 seconds.

- Boil water in a medium saucepan. Add edamame and cook dinner 1 to 2 minutes. Drain edamame and rinse under bloodless water to save you it from cooking similarly.

- Add cooked edamame, tahini, garlic, olive oil, cilantro, and lemon juice to a food processor or blender and pulse till smooth. Add salt and pepper to taste.

- Serve right now or switch to an hermetic field. Hummus may be stored up to 3 days within the fridge.

GRILLED GINGER CHICKEN

This grilled chicken entrée makes for a heart-healthy dinner full of scrumptious flavor. The clean ginger may additionally help calm your belly whilst your digestion is off.

Ingredients

- 4 4-ounce boneless, skinless bird breasts

- ¼ teaspoon black pepper

- Cooking spray

- 1 tablespoon peanut oil

- 1 ¼ cup scallions, thinly sliced

- 1 ½ tablespoons clean ginger, peeled and grated

- 3 tablespoons sweet sherry

- 3 tablespoons low-sodium hen inventory

- ½ tablespoon oyster sauce

- 2 teaspoons rice vinegar

Instructions

- Pat bird breasts dry and sprinkle with

  pepper.

- Lightly coat a grill pan with cooking spray

  and heat over medium-excessive

  warmness. Add hen to pan and grill 5-6

  minutes on every aspect.

- While chook is cooking, heat peanut oil in

  a separate skillet over medium-excessive

  warmness.

- Add 1 cup scallions and the ginger. Cook

  for 2 mins.

- Add sherry, inventory, and oyster sauce to ginger and scallions and cook dinner for some other minute.

- Stir in rice vinegar and warmth thru.

- Pour sauce over chook and serve heat. Garnish with last scallions.

HERBED AVOCADO EGG SALAD

Replace the mayonnaise with avocado and creamy nonfat Greek yogurt and you've got an egg salad this is heart healthy and secure for people following a low-fiber eating regimen. Top on a slide of bread or serve with salad vegetables.

Ingredients

- 10 eggs

- 1 avocado

- ½ cup nonfat simple Greek yogurt

- ½ teaspoon Dijon mustard

- Juice of one lemon

- 1 tablespoon chopped chives

- 1 tablespoon chopped dill

- Salt and pepper

- 1 tablespoon olive oil

Instructions

- Place eggs in a saucepan and fill with water so eggs are covered. Bring to a boil, then eliminate from warmth and let eggs rest in water for 8 to 10 minutes. Remove eggs from pan and run underneath cold water. Cool and peel, discarding shells.

- Mash avocado and eggs collectively until a textured and chunky in consistency. Add yogurt, mustard, lemon juice, and herbs. Season with salt and pepper to taste. Drizzle with olive oil.

- Serve chilled or at room temperature. Transfer salad to a bowl if serving immediately or to an hermetic field if saving for later. Store up to 3 days within the fridge.

LEMON CHICKEN

You don't want highly-priced elements to put together a flavorful and scrumptious hen dish. The trick is to marinate the chicken beforehand of time so that the lemon and spices infuse the beef. Serve with pasta, rice, or cauliflower rice.

Ingredients

- Juice of two lemons
- 2 tablespoons greater-virgin olive oil
- 2 teaspoons lemon pepper
- 1 teaspoon dried basil
- 1 teaspoon dried oregano
- ¼ teaspoon salt
- 4 boneless, skinless bird breasts

- 4 tablespoons sparkling parsley, chopped (elective)

- 4 lemon slices (non-compulsory)

Instructions

- Combine lemon juice, olive oil, lemon pepper, basil, oregano, and salt in a resealable gallon-length plastic bag. Add hen breasts to bag and shake to coat. Marinate within the fridge as a minimum 30 minutes and up to 8 hours.

- Heat a heavy skillet over medium-high warmness. Add hen to skillet; discard marinade. Cook 6 to 7 minutes on every aspect. Temperature of chicken need to be a hundred sixty five levels the usage of an instantaneous-study thermometer.

- Garnish with parsley and lemon slices, if desired.

MONTREAL-RUBBED SALMON

Adding dried or fresh herbs on your food is a high-quality manner to lessen salt with out dropping flavor. This heart-healthy dish gets its name from Montreal spice rub, a mix of garlic, coriander, black pepper, cayenne, and dill.

Ingredients

- ½ tablespoon Montreal steak seasoning

- 1 tablespoon dark brown sugar

- 4 salmon filets (6 oz every), skin eliminated

- Grapeseed or coconut oil cooking spray

Instructions

- Preheat oven to four hundred tiers.

- In small bowl, combine seasoning and brown sugar. Rub combination into each salmon filet.

- Lightly coat sheet pan with cooking spray. Place fish on prepared pan and bake till inner temperature reaches 145 degrees using a meat thermometer, about 12 to fifteen minutes. Let fish relaxation 2 mins before serving.

OVEN-BAKED CHICKEN FAJITAS

Serve this energizing dish with flour or corn tortillas or on a bed of brown rice. The portion for the Carbohydrate Controlled eating regimen is two 6-inch tortillas or half a cup of brown rice.

Ingredients

- 1 tablespoon chili powder
- ½ tablespoon paprika
- ½ teaspoon onion powder
- ¼ teaspoon garlic powder
- ¼ teaspoon floor cumin
- ⅛ teaspoon cayenne pepper
- 1 teaspoon sugar

- ½ teaspoon salt

- 1 massive onion, sliced in ¼-inch-

  extensive strips

- 3 bell peppers, any coloration, sliced in ¼-

  inch-extensive strips

- 1 pound boneless, skinless hen breast,

  sliced in ¼-inch-wide strips

- 2 tablespoons vegetable oil

- Juice of half a lime

- 8 6-inch tortillas (flour or corn)

- ½ cup bitter cream (optionally available)

- ¼ bunch sparkling cilantro (optional)

Instructions

- Thoroughly rinse sparkling produce under warm running water for 20 seconds. Scrub to cast off extra dust.

- Preheat oven to four hundred tiers.

- Mix the chili powder, paprika, onion powder, garlic powder, cumin, cayenne, sugar, and salt in a small bowl and set aside.

- Spread onions and bell peppers in a 13x15 casserole dish or on a big rimmed baking sheet. Top with sliced bird. Drizzle oil over chook and greens, then sprinkle seasoning mixture on top. Toss till blended. Bake 35 to forty mins, stirring as soon as halfway thru. Temperature of fajitas must be one hundred sixty five stages the use of an immediate-read thermometer.

- Sprinkle lime juice over fajitas and serve without delay with tortillas and, if the use of, bitter cream and cilantro.

OVERNIGHT OATS

Overnight oats make for an energizing, iron- and protein-wealthy breakfast. Top with peanut butter or sliced almonds for extra protein.

Ingredients

- ⅓ cup rolled oats

- ½ cup low-fat milk

- ⅓ cup nonfat simple yogurt (Greek or normal)

- ½ cup unsweetened applesauce

- 1 teaspoon cinnamon

- 1 teaspoon brown sugar

Instructions

- Combine all substances in a bowl and permit soak overnight in refrigerator. Stir nicely earlier than serving.

QUINOA SALAD

This salad is filled with fiber and healthful fat.

Feel unfastened to use any entire grain in region of quinoa to mix it up at the same time as nonetheless keeping the coronary heart

advantages. You can also alternative other

unsalted nuts or dried fruits.

This salad is packed with fiber and healthful fats.

Feel free to apply any entire grain in location of

quinoa to mix it up at the same time as

nonetheless keeping the heart advantages. You

can also substitute other unsalted nuts or dried

culmination.

Ingredients

- ½ cup quinoa

- 1 cup water

- 1 14.Four-ounce bag frozen stir-fry

  vegetables

- 1 tablespoon chopped walnuts

- ¼ cup raisins

- 1 tablespoon olive oil

- 1 tablespoon olive oil

- 1 teaspoon curry powder

Instructions

- In small pot over medium-excessive warmth, bring quinoa and water to a boil. Reduce warmness to medium low, cowl, and simmer until liquid is completely absorbed, 10 to 20 minutes. Remove pot from heat, maintaining it blanketed, and permit stand five minutes. Uncover and fluff quinoa with a fork.

- Steam or microwave frozen vegetables according to package deal guidelines.

- Combine quinoa, vegetables, and remaining components in huge bowl and serve.

QUINOA SALAD WITH FETA

This zesty, versatile dish can be served as a aspect, appetizer, or maybe the bottom of a hearty salad.

Ingredients

- 2 cups quinoa

- 3½ cups low-sodium chook or vegetable broth

- 1 cup grape tomatoes, halved

- ⅔ cup chopped clean parsley

- ½ cup diced cucumber, peeled and seeded

- ½ cup minced red onions

- four ounces feta cheese, crumbled

- 3 tablespoons olive oil

- three tablespoons red wine vinegar

- 2 cloves garlic, minced

- Juice of one lemon

- Salt and pepper

Instructions

- Thoroughly rinse fresh produce beneath warm walking water for 20 seconds. Scrub to cast off excess dust.

- Rinse quinoa in a high-quality-mesh colander underneath strolling water for as a minimum 30 seconds. Drain well.

- In a saucepan, carry rinsed quinoa and broth to a boil. Reduce heat to medium-low, cowl, and simmer until quinoa is smooth and broth is absorbed, 15 to twenty minutes. Transfer to a large bowl and set apart to chill.

- Add tomatoes, parsley, cucumber, onions, feta, olive oil, vinegar, and garlic to cooled quinoa and mix to mix. Pour lemon juice over quinoa salad and season with salt and pepper to taste. Toss to coat and refrigerate until prepared to serve.

- Washing the quinoa properly earlier than cooking allows to get rid of bitterness because of naturally taking place saponins. Saponins are chemical compounds located in quinoa and other plant-based totally meals, and had been shown to possess a number of fitness advantages.

RED CABBAGE SLAW

This cabbage salad has a tangy tropical twist with crunchy chopped jicama and juicy mango slices. Jicama is a root vegetable that is wealthy in vitamins and minerals. If you could't discover it in shops, red bell pepper works well as a substitution.

Ingredients

- Cooking spray

- ½ cup pepitas or pumpkin seeds

- ½ cup sunflower seeds

- ½ head red cabbage, sliced thinly

- ½ jicama, peeled and chopped

- 1 mango (company), sliced

- ¼ to ½ cup cilantro, chopped

- ½ cup pepitas or pumpkin seeds, toasted

- ½ cup sunflower seeds, toasted

- Juice from 2 limes

- ¼ cup rice wine vinegar

- 2 tablespoons honey

- ¼ cup more-virgin olive oil

- Salt

Instructions

- Thoroughly rinse fresh produce beneath warm jogging water for 20 seconds. Scrub to put off excess dirt.

- Coat a skillet with cooking spray and toast seeds till brown, approximately 10 mins.

- Combine toasted seeds, cabbage, jicama, mango, cilantro, lime juice, vinegar, honey, and olive oil in a massive bowl. Add salt to flavor.

- Serve straight away or switch to an hermetic box. Slaw can be saved up to three days inside the fridge.

SALMON FILLET WITH YOGURT AVOCADO SAUCE

Try this baked fish whilst you're low on strength. The creamy avocado sauce is delicious and can assist in case you're having problems swallowing.

Ingredients

- 1 avocado

- ½ cup Greek yogurt

- three tablespoons cilantro leaves

- 1 clove garlic

- 2 tablespoons lemon juice

- 1 tablespoon water, plus greater as needed

- 1 teaspoon salt, plus more for seasoning

- 1 teaspoon ground pepper, plus extra for seasoning

- four 3-ounce salmon fillets

- 1 tablespoons olive oil

Instructions

- Preheat oven to four hundred ranges. Line a baking sheet with aluminum foil.

- Combine avocado, yogurt, cilantro, garlic, lemon juice, 1 tablespoon water, and 1 teaspoon each salt and pepper in a meals processor and mix till smooth. If essential, add more water, 1 tablespoon at a time, until sauce reaches preferred consistency.

- Place fish skin-facet down on prepared baking sheet. Season with salt and pepper and brush with olive oil. Bake fish till simply cooked via, 8 to ten mins. Fish have to sign in 145 tiers Fahrenheit the use of an immediate-read thermometer within the center of the fillet.

- Serve fish crowned with sauce.

SPICED CHICKPEAS

The next time you're yearning potato chips reach for this addictive snack alternatively. The key's to make certain that the chickpeas are thoroughly dried earlier than you pop them within the oven.

The chickpeas should appearance stupid in look

after you blot them with paper towels.

Ingredients

- 1 teaspoon floor cumin

- 1 teaspoon smoked candy paprika

- ½ teaspoon garlic powder

- ½ teaspoon onion powder

- ⅛ teaspoon salt

- ⅛ teaspoon black pepper

- Pinch of cayenne pepper

- 2 tablespoons more-virgin olive oil

- 1 15-ounce can chickpeas, no salt

  delivered or low sodium, drained

Instructions

- Preheat oven to 400 levels.

- In a medium mixing bowl, use a small whisk to combine cumin, paprika, garlic powder, onion powder, salt, black pepper, and cayenne. Add oil and whisk to combine.

- Place a double layer of paper towels on a piece surface. Rinse chickpeas in a colander. Shake nicely, then spread chickpeas evenly across paper towels. Blot chickpeas using a smooth paper towel. Repeat as needed, till chickpeas are thoroughly dry.

- Add chickpeas to spice mixture and, the usage of your fingers, gently blend and rubdown till they are calmly coated.

- Line a baking sheet with parchment paper and spread chickpeas flippantly throughout pan.

- Bake, rotating sheet every 8 mins, until chickpeas are company, 24 to 32 mins.

- Remove sheet from oven and permit chickpeas to chill. Serve without delay or switch to an airtight field. Chickpeas may be stored up to a few days within the refrigerator.

SWEET POTATO HASH

This wholesome, fulfilling dish works properly for some of unique diets. Enjoy it with own family or friends over brunch.

Ingredients

- 2 tablespoons olive oil
- four sweet potatoes, peeled and shredded
- 1 bunch kale, chopped
- Salt and pepper
- Cooking spray
- 6 eggs

Instructions

- Thoroughly rinse sparkling produce underneath heat walking water for 20 seconds. Scrub to remove extra dust.

- Preheat oven to 350 ranges.

- Heat a massive skillet over high warmness. Add olive oil and shredded sweet potato and cook until smooth, about 10 mins. Add kale and cook until wilted. Season mixture with salt and pepper to taste.

- Coat a 9x13 baking dish with cooking spray. Spoon sweet potato combination into prepared dish. Then, the use of a spoon, make 6 wells inside the combination, spaced frivolously around the dish, and crack an egg into each one. Top with a sprinkle of salt and pepper.

- Bake till eggs are cooked and yolks are set. Internal temperature of the hash should be a hundred and sixty degrees the usage of an instant-read thermometer. Serve right now.

TURKEY SAGE MEATLOAF

Turkey meatloaf is a awesome desire if you're looking to hold calories in check and your coronary heart healthy. Shown here with a side of ginger candy potato slices.

Ingredients

- 1 tablespoon grapeseed oil

- 1 small onion, chopped

- 2 stalks celery, chopped

- 1 tablespoon garlic, chopped

- ½ cup Italian parsley, chopped

- 3 tablespoons sage, chopped

- 3 kilos lean floor turkey

- 2 eggs

- 1 tablespoon salt

- Black pepper to taste

- 1 ⅓ cups panko bread crumbs

- 16 ounces low-sodium gravy of desire

Instructions

- Preheat oven to 375 stages.

- Heat oil in a huge frying pan. Add onion, celery, and garlic. Cook over medium warmth 5 to 7 mins, stirring frequently, until combination is soft but not browned.

- Remove pan from heat and let cool.

- Transfer mixture to an extra-massive bowl. Stir in parsley and sage. Add ground turkey, eggs, salt, pepper, and panko bread crumbs and blend to combine.

- Place combination in baking dish. Form into a loaf with moist hands. Bake 60 to 65 mins or till inner temperature reaches a hundred sixty five levels. Serve with warm gravy.

www.ingramcontent.com/pod-product-compliance
Lightning Source LLC
Chambersburg PA
CBHW052119150726
48002CB00006B/2419